Emotional Manipulation Tactics

37 Covert Tactics Manipulators & Narcissists Use To Control Relationships

The Guidebook To Guard Against Dark Psychology

NESA LONG

DEDICATION

For my best friend, Cindy…

Celebrating your freedom from years of manipulation!

TABLE OF CONTENTS

INTRODUCTION

"Because to take away a man's freedom of choice, even his freedom to make the wrong choice, is to manipulate him as though he were a puppet and not a person."

— Madeline L'Engle

Manipulative people could be anyone: Father, mother, boyfriend, girlfriend, wife, husband, sister, brother, mother in-law, sister-in law, brother-in-law, son, daughter, friend, boss, employee, colleagues and neighbors. These are people who know how to scare, criticize, bribe, coerce, offer sympathy, guilt trip, flatter, obligate, intimidate, undermine, act innocent, blame or abuse in order to seize power in a relationship and ultimately control the other person.

We all have legitimate needs for emotional wellbeing and physical survival. It is normal to strive to meet these needs by interacting with others in a fair and balanced way, towards a favorable outcome for everyone. This is what healthy people do. Manipulative people, on the other hand, deceitfully seek to influence someone in order to benefit themselves in some way. It involves control and coercion.

Manipulation can be healthy or unhealthy. Manipulation is healthy when done occasionally. Besides, everyone manipulates others from time to time. For instance, we are bombarded with adverts from the media and from the internet; which are generally designed to influence our thoughts in a bid to advance the advertiser's cause. A parent manipulates their child into eating vegetables; a police negotiator uses manipulation at a bank hostage situation; a motivator speaker also, to make people happier. Even babies are not left out, however innocuous theirs may be. They cry and throw tantrums to elicit your favorable response or reactions.

Manipulation becomes unhealthy and toxic when it is done in order to be cruel and malicious. It is unhealthy when it is done habitually and persistently, and when it becomes the abuser's only way to get what they want. It is also unhealthy when exerting control and power over others becomes a way of life. Disturbingly, this form of abuse is prevalent in our personal and professional lives. Some are open and easy to identify, but many are covert and subtle, wounding our emotions and self-esteem.

No one deserves to be manipulated and if you a victim, it's isn't your fault. The most important thing is to recognize them quickly and be free of them as soon as possible for your sanity, value and dignity.

This is what this book is all about.

Chapter One

Understanding Emotional Manipulation

"Until you realize how easy it is for your mind to be manipulated, you remain the puppet of someone else's game."

— Evita Ochel

Emotional manipulation involves the direct or indirect control of another person's actions or behavior. It is a covert and subtle art of making demands and threats to get what you want. It is a dysfunctional and unhealthy form of manipulation that is frustrating and debilitating. It is mentally and emotionally exhausting.

Emotional manipulators use mind games to seize power in a relationship. They exude confidence and are usually charismatic. They know how to read people to know those who are highly sympathetic and those prone to emotional responses, like crying at movies or loving puppies. They are relaxed and seldom anxious. They appear caring, defending and vulnerable, especially at first appearance, but are masters at using your vulnerabilities against you.

Passive aggressive people who avoid direct confrontations are usually covertly aggressive. They say and do things such as lying, acting caring or shocked in order to get what they want. The manipulator is an actor; he know just the words to say and the non-verbal response to take; such as, shedding a sudden tear or two, or having an impromptu fit of rage, to suit his needs at that moment.

These disturbed personalities are usually spiteful and deceitful. Their goal is simply power – at your expense. Psychopathic manipulators want to meet their need for power and control. Narcissists manipulate to satisfy their need for approval, admiration and attention. People without serious psychological disorders use manipulation from time to time to attain their selfish pursuits.   They know how to play the manipulative 'game' on their significant other and others they come in contact with.

While they are at it, they hide their aggressive intent, deny their self-serving motives, and ruthlessly seek their objectives of making you doubt yourself and your perception. After a while, they become skilled emotional manipulators who enjoy the control that they have gotten and are unwilling to relinquish it.

Unfortunately, when the manipulation is happening to you, it is usually hard to spot. So these emotional abusers are often able to get away with it, until after the damage has been done. It is also hard to detect because our emotional attachments can affect our perception or judgment.

Why People Manipulate

1. **Learned behavior**

People learn manipulation when they are young. Parents who use threats and guilt to achieve their purpose may end up passing this manipulative threats to their children. Manipulative people are usually narcissists who have been manipulated by their parents or caregivers when they were kids. Parents need to set acceptable standard of behavior for their children. A kid who knows his mother will disapprove of an action will go straight to his dad who is likely to say yes. This is manipulation.

2. **Unhealed Wounds**

Others manipulate because of their own pain and woundedness. They experienced some traumatic, unfortunate or troublesome event in the past which tore away their conscience and they begin to see others as tools for their own advantage. For instance, someone with a fear of abandonment would do anything to ensure that their partner *needs* them in order to avoid being abandoned. It is what we fear that we manifest into our relationships, most of the time. Manipulative people anxiously react to situations instead of to simply relate.

Manipulative people do not consciously plan their maneuvers. Rather, they come from a personality disorder within them that are played out within the context of the other person who entertains the manipulator and unknowingly fuels the manipulation.

These personality disorders are: **Narcissistic Personality Disorder (NPD):** Someone with a mental illness known as Narcissistic Personality Disorder has a strong preoccupation of his own power and prestige. They have a high sense of superiority and an intense longing to be admired. They have little or no sympathy, empathy and conscience. They manipulate themselves out of a bad situation, thinking it's the normal way of life. To them, the ends justifies the means.

Borderline Personality Disorder (BPD): These people are highly sensitive to rejection and abandonment and so resort to manipulative control to avoid it.

It takes years of mental treatment to be rid of these two personality disorders.

Most manipulative individuals share four common characteristics:

1. They can detect your weaknesses.

2. They use the detected weaknesses against you.

3. They convince you to let go something of yours in order to serve their self-centered interests.

4. They will keep at the manipulation until you become aware of it and take action to stop it.

They use fear, guilt and blame to make others feel guilty, ashamed or deprive them of their own happiness.

Emotional abuse/manipulation should never be encouraged. It completely disregards someone's value and dignity. Abusive behavior impacts heavily and negatively on a person. The victim suffers emotionally, physically and spiritually. It causes mental stress and fatigue, anxiety and depression. It leads to feelings to shame and helplessness as well as a compromised self-confidence.

This is why you need to study tactics and techniques of abuse so you can easily identify them. This way, you will be better prepared to protect yourself from abuse and exploitation, set boundaries and make sound decisions about who to let into your life. That said, these 37 covert emotional manipulation tactics will get you prepared.

Chapter Two

37 Emotional Manipulation Tactics

Love Bombing

"I know we've just met, but I can't wait to move in with you!"

Shower a person with a superfluity of affection and attention and the person will feel on top of the world. These include public display of affection, gifts and compliments, intense sex, appreciation, adoration and flattery, profuse apologies, public recognition and constant text messaging. However, the aim of all these is to create dependency, gain power and control. This is love bombing. It is a form of abuse.

The love bomber creates a fast-moving, passionate and exhilarating relationship that leaves you with butterflies in your stomach. They are full of promises for the future, tell you the relationship is destined and call you their soulmate. You may have planned to have an easy, slow and steady relationship, but you soon find yourself entangled in a serious relationship; doing the exact opposite and thinking that you are both made for one another.

However, the excessive flattery, over-the top gifts, and constant texting comes with a price: your recognition, worship and reward. For example, they want prompt response to text messages. When you fail to return the level of affection that you're being shown, they'll get mad; label you uncaring and this is when you'll start to see another character that's mean, self-centered and unreasonable. A simple phone call from a family in the middle of a date could really piss them off!

Love bombing is dangerous because it makes you lose your sense of self. It is harmful because it creates the false belief that the narcissist is open and vulnerable. This makes you feel at ease, causing you to open up more than usual, and leaving room for more control and manipulation. The tactic is to build you up and then throw you off the pedestal without warning! After the love, comes the bombshell! Compliments will cease and be replaced by belittling insults that'll devalue and erode your esteem.

This is a covert tactic because it is difficult to detect from the beginning. So how do you differentiate genuine attention from love bombing? If you just met someone and you are now being called a soulmate and receiving a constant declaration of underlying love, be careful. You can only test its genuineness if the action continues and it is matched by their words.

What to do: Listen to your guts: it'll tell you something's off. If a relationship is going too fast, be bold and tell your partner to take it slow, and to give the relationship more time to develop. A lovebomber will try to brush off your feelings, make excuses or become offended at the idea. Lay off!

<u>**Traumatic Bonding**</u>

'I don't know why he wouldn't speak to me for days; but that's ok now… he brought me flowers!'

Traumatic bonding is a powerful manipulate tactic that keeps you trauma bonded to your abuser who plays with your feelings. Also known as intermittent reinforcement, it involves employing small acts of kindness, or periodic affection to gain control of someone else's emotions. One minute you are elated and ecstatic at the attention you are receiving, and the wonderful feeling you are having. The next minute, it ends and you become doubtful, anxious and upset.

Sporadic acts of kindness such as getting flowers after a few days of silent treatment or a surprise gift after an outburst, causes us to mistrust our instincts about the motive and genuine character of the disturbed personality. This way, we are more likely to accept their sob tales after abusive incidents.

The unpredictability of the abuse cycle fuels the victim's dependency. You feel you are doing something wrong, but cannot pinpoint what you may be doing wrong to warrant being treated in this manner. You may even feel like you are overreacting sometimes. Confrontations lead to denial which may reassure you for a while, but it's not enough, as the manipulator persists on providing intermittent reinforcement in order to place you in a state of dependency and control.

What to do: Understand that you're dealing with a narcissist and create distance in the form of no contact or no contact. Get in touch with a trauma-experienced professional to help you remain detached from your abuser.

<u>Projection</u>

"If I can do it, then you can as well!"

This diversionary tactics involves taking a negative aspect of oneself and projecting it on a person or situation. Manipulators use this defense mechanism to absolve themselves of responsibility and then turn around and project those responsibilities on someone else. They do not want to take the blame for their errors but seeks to place the guilt burden on another.

In your life's journey, you may know or have heard about individuals who behave like this. This person wants what 'everyone' wants. It is always 'John and the guys' who are saying 'this is the way to do it'. But when you really look into it, John never did say anything like that. Another example is the lazy work employee who blames the management for firing him; instead of accepting that his indolence and consistence poor performance contributed to the company's rising debt profile and the resulting staff layoff.

Abusers will use projection to accuse you of the things they themselves are guilty of; and they will do this often until you start to feel guilty and ashamed for your supposed 'poor and irresponsible' decisions. To them, you have a hand in every lousy situation. Once there is a problem or an issue is identified, you must have played a role in bringing it about.

Manipulators plant their ideas in your mind and then let you believe that it was your idea all along. *"Do you think we should go on holiday soon? I've heard Hawaii is nice this time of year…"*

Emotional manipulators who use projection as a tactic, have very poor self-insight and will never take responsibility for an action. They views a mirror as though it were a window. Sadly, this is the way a projector views life, and the world at large. They accuse someone else of being controlling or racist when it is they themselves that are being controlling or being racist.

Note that the projector is not conscious of this action. It is an action that has gone unchecked for a long time and has become habitual. People who easily detect other's faults are only projecting their negative selves. Blaming others is the only way they can justify their own behaviors.

What to do? Having identified this tactic, do not take action on just what the manipulator says without confirming. Do not make promises as well. When they plant their ideas into your mind, ask that they repeat their point. Ask for clarity. Also repeat their point in your words. Narcissists are worse; they have to interest in change or self-insight. Simply cut ties with them as soon as possible.

<u>**Minimizing**</u>

"It's really wasn't that bad, get over it!"

Manipulators who use minimizing as a tactic acknowledges that they may have done something wrong but trivialize or minimize the level of the wrong or harm done, making the results of their action seem less harmful than it really is.

At first it may seem that people who minimize the outcome of their action did so because they felt bad about it. It seemed that they were convicted of their wrongs by their conscience so much that they had to trivialize their actions in order to live with themselves. But professionals have proven that the primary reason these character-impaired individuals minimize is to manage the impression others have of them. They do not want you to see them for the flawed character that they are. They also want to convince you that your perception about their actions are wrong. This is why the aggressive manipulator will minimize his action by saying something like *"I just pushed her a bit!"*

They resist accountability by convincing you that the wrongful action taken aren't as bad and harmful as they know it, or as you think it was. Once they make you think or perceive that they aren't such a bad person by their actions, they have succeeded in managing the impressions you have of them; and also in manipulating you.

The skilled manipulator who admits that part of his actions were wrong will usually concede to the less serious parts, leaving out the major ones. But conceding a point or two is not the same as taking full responsibility for the wrongdoing.

The danger of minimizing is that since the individual does not consider a particular problem as a serious one, there is zero chance of addressing or correcting the problem. Whatever wrong they did are usually 'not as bad", as others or what they did in the past. If someone cannot accept his faults wholly, they will certainly do it again. As they constantly avoid responsibility and manipulate, they place undue stress on you.

What to do? Point out how you feel about the action instead of arguing about the other's person attempt at minimizing the action. However, when someone keeps justifying a behavior that causes you hurt and pain, this may be just the right time for you to seek professional help.

Victimization

"At least you have a brother. I've felt alone all my life."

The emotional manipulator plays the victim. No matter what happens, they manage to portray themselves as victims of someone else circumstance or behavior. This is the *poor me* individual who manipulatively always want to appear powerless in order to get the other party to succumb to their wishes and demands. They are the *"Nobody likes me"*, and *"Everybody hates me"* character who hates to be accountable for anything.

Nothing is ever their fault, no matter what they do or didn't do. This person often gets mad or upset, but manages to pin the fault on you for upsetting them. It's your fault for also having unreasonable expectations. In all the constant arguments and fights they usually instigate, they are often the victim. The tactic is to make you feel guilty.

They engage in emotional battles with their partner or with others, making them feel guilty for even the actions they take by emphasizing their own poor me emotional state. It's worse if manipulator has suffered a setback; they will bring this up especially when you are having a good time. They may say things like *"I feel embarrassed for you whenever I see you play with Annie's kids as though they were ours – and it's all because we never had children"*. Or the twice- divorced single woman who constantly bickers will say to her married sister, *"you will not understand what I want, you are happily married, you have two kids!*

After spats, you find yourself constantly apologizing while the other person plays the victim, even though you've both been hurt by each other's actions. They are always hurt and helpless and in need of extra love and attention. They also enjoy getting sympathy from people around them such as neighbors, coworkers and friends, and enjoy turning people against each other.

The victim also feels entitled in some way. The victims feels angry that that he is not in charge of his responsibility so they project their anger at others. They frequently accuse others of betrayal and never accept personal responsibility for their actions.

If you a very compassionate and sympathetic person, they will try to convince you that they are suffering is some way e.g. have lost their job, their partner left them. You'll try to help them get relieve form their distress in some way and find yourself entangled in their victimization.

What to do? Try not to respond to guilt and simply apologize for the actions that you feel you should apologize for, and insist that you will not apologize for the other. Do not be moved by tears, threats, or blackmail.

<u>**Negative Reinforcement**</u>

This is the reward or incentive an abuser offers for the removal of the action they finds unpleasant, undesirable or uncomfortable. So, once you yield to the manipulator's demands, they will stop acting in a negative manner. For instance, coming home late.

In the future, if you want your partner to come home early etc., you will do what you did the first time. What this means is that you are being conditioned through the negative reinforces the manipulator deliberately introduces.

Another example of negative reinforcement is can be seen between parents and kids. A child who doesn't want to wear a certain shirt and knows their mum will not have them wear damaged clothes cuts the shirts with scissors and the mum on seeing this damage, takes the shirt away. In future, the child will damage the shirts they do not want to wear.

<u>**Gaslighting**</u>

"Are you sure? You tend to forget a lot."

Gaslighting is a coercive and serious form of emotional abuse. It is used by very skilled manipulators, including narcissists and psychopaths, to make you think you are wrong even when you are right, causing you to question your own mental wellbeing, feelings and thoughts. This is the aim anyway: to make you begin to question your own perception of reality with the conclusion that your own instincts and thoughts cannot be trusted. It can occur in personal or professional relationship.

It is subtle at the beginning, with the gaslighter convincing you that their version of events in the truth. Instead of questioning the manipulator unreasonable behavior, you start to question yourself. For instance, you know he said he will pay for half the groceries. You remember clearly because you were happy about it. Now he denies it so vigorously, firmly and innocently that you are left confused.

The gaslighter begins by changing small details in stories. The aim is to gain dominance in the relationship. Gaslighters usually refuse to listen to what you have to say and go on to accuse you of being the one confusing issues, they pretend to not understand your perceptive, and resort to a lie, such as "That never happened," and then counter your logical sequence of events.

Constant gaslighting will make you feel depressed, anxious and confused but you won't be able to pinpoint these feelings. You will feel you can't do anything right, and you may be forced to lie just to avoid hurtful comments. Words, emotions and experiences are constantly being twisted, leading to a gradual loss of self-confidence and a greater dependence on the abuser.

This tactic is a 'crazy- making one' because the abuser repeatedly insist or imply that your perception of a situation is unreal or nonsensical, making you believe you're crazy. By successfully creating doubts in minds of others, gaslighters increase their power and control over them.

Some of their common statements include:

- *"Don't you think you're over-reacting?"*
- *"I know what you're thinking."*
- *"Were you even paying attention?"*
- *"You have no sense of humor"*
- *"You always jump to the wrong conclusion."*
- *"If you were paying attention…"*
- *"You're reading too much into this."*
- *"You're too sensitive."*
- *"Why would you even think that?"*
- *"You're taking this too personally,"*
- *"You're being dramatic."*
- *"We talked about this. Don't you remember?"*

Gaslighting is very dangerous because it is subtle and covert. It may takes years to realize that you are a victim. Gaslighting is also difficult to prove because legally it must be established that there is a threat of physical violence or the other person's behavior is impeding heavily on your daily life. It can happen to anyone: family members, close friends or employees.

You may be a victim of gaslighting if you:

- Question whether you can do anything right
- Are constantly in self-doubt and constantly second-guess yourself.
- Wonder if you are too sensitive
- Feel confused and ask yourself if you are "going crazy"
- Question whether you are "good enough" for your partner
- Find it difficult to make simple decisions
- Create your own lies and half trusts in order to escape being put down

What to do:

Learn to recognize the signs and patterns, do not let anyone invalidate your feelings. Remember that your perceptive is important and your opinions must be heard and respected.

What to say to a gaslighter:

"I hear you and that isn't my experience."

"We remember things differently."

"If you continue to speak to me like this; I'm not engaging."

You can also deal with it by insisting on writing everything down, this will throw the gaslighter off guard but insist on it. Say something like: *"sorry, but I just need to write this down"*. When the abuser senses that you are serious about this, they are likely to backpedal. Besides, keeping track of your words and action will restore your confidence and make you less dependence. Writing also helps if the abuser is your boss.

If possible, you can cut all ties with the gaslighter: resign and get a new job, leave home or break up with your partner. By creating a bit of distance, you will keep safe.

<u>**Silent Treatment/ Withholding**</u>

"My dad wouldn't speak to me; it's been 6 weeks now!

Silence treatment also called withholding and has to do with holding back communication, response, positive feedback, agreement, acknowledgement and acceptance. It is an emotional abuse aimed at manipulating someone else into submission.

It is not restricted to only partners in relationships, as it cuts across every sphere of relationship, including between friends, co-workers, as well as between parents and children. Studies have shown that the act of ignoring triggers the same area of the brain that detects physical pain. So we could even say it's worse than physical abuse because it inflicts emotional pain without bruising. The silent treatment comes up as a response to conflict in a relationship. It is used as a passive-aggressive form of control.

In some cases, going silent might be the best action to take in a particular situation, so as not to say things you might regret later. But it becomes abusive and manipulative when it is used to exert power and create emotional distance. Withholding conversation is a tactic of gaining superiority and control.

When someone remains silent for a lengthy period of time, you'll start to imagine several things you may have said wrong or done wrong. Soon you'll be blaming yourself for bringing about the silent treatment. The silence treatment indicates a lack of respect and value for others. It is intended to hurt. It contributes to depression, and low self-esteem. It is frustrating and may cause you to lose your self-esteem by constantly seeking for their attention. It can make you feel rejected or excluded. The manipulator wants you to plead, apologize or give in to demands.

What to do: The good news is that this tactic is not covert. It is apparent and can be effectively tackled. Once you recognize that you are being given the silent treatment, let the manipulator know that you are aware of being given the silent treatment.

However, add that you have made a decision not to let this action bother you but you are ready whenever they are to talk things over. Once you've made this known, go about your duties and tasks without letting it bother you. Simply act like it's really no big deal. By this response and attitude, the issue will soon be resolved and you have effectively weakened this tactics, it will not be used against you anymore.

Remember do not:

- Beg or plead because it encourages the behavior
- Respond in anger because it can make things worse.
- Apologize because you did nothing wrong
- Take it personally because you are not to blame for the way others treat you
- Threaten to end the relationship if you really didn't plan to.

Diversion

Well, what about Susie? Don't you remember that time when…?"

An experienced manipulator finds it hard to focus on a single line of discussion without diverting. An unfavorable subject is immediately redirected once the abuser finds it uncomfortable and unfavorable. Without you noticing, your attention is skillfully moved elsewhere.it shows up in sentences like *"What about the time when…"* Abusers use this tactic to take your attention off them and their behavior. They use circular conversation, flattery, lie or point attention to other people you know with worse actions.

Talk about their inability to hold a job, and they will remind you about the terrible way your mother treated them at thanksgiving and how are they supposed to work after that? Complain about their neglectful parenting and you'll hear about a mistake you made six years ago.

It plays out in the workplace as well. You approach a skilled manipulator to call out an error or correct behavior. They immediately point out a crisis that requires your prompt attention. There is no limit to their diversionary tactics in terms of time and subject.

What to do: Do not be derailed. Keep stating the facts without succumbing to their distractions. Instead say *"That's not what I am talking about"* and redirect their redirection. Tell them to stay focus on the issue at hand. If they aren't interested in what you have to say, simply walk away and expend your energy on someone or something more constructive.

Evasion/ Generalization

Evasion is closely relation to diversion. Manipulators do not like answering specific questions that they find unfavorable. Instead they will evade your question by providing you with a broad view of issues. They prefer to give unclear, irrelevant and rambling responses instead of answering a direct question. Narcissists or psychopaths do not like being challenged and so use words like bullets to steer you off the truth they do not want you to know. The aim to distract, confuse and frustrate you.

Emotional Blackmail

Do it or else …!

Manipulators want you to yield to their demands. They issue ultimatums and make dramatic statements to get you yielding to their demand.

E.g. *"I'll kill myself if you leave."* Or do it in a more subtle manner, *"If you can't be here this weekend, I think it shows your level of dedication to this office."*

Most of these statements are usually made to elicit apology.

What to do: try not to yield or apologize. Once you yield, they have succeeded in using fear, shame or guilt to their advantage.

The (un)Willing Helper

Most manipulators rarely say no when asked to do something. They may offer a reluctant yes or a high-sounding yes, depending on their mood. However, when they do perform the action, they lace it with non-verbal signs and body languages to indicate that it is far from a pleasant experience.

Heavy sighs, rolling eyes, a pissed off facial expression all show that they are helping but unwilling. When you point out this out, they will vehemently deny, call you 'unreasonable' and make it all about you. Furthermore, they will ensure that everyone knows about the help they've rendered so that they can easily ask for something bigger and more valuable next time.

What to do: Make their YES stand. A yes from a potential manipulator should be accounted for. Do not be fooled by the sighs or non-verbal cues that accompany it to indicate that they really do not want to do it. If they do not want to do something, you should be told.

Furthermore, don't be afraid to say no, when they ask you for a favor. You don't need to help them if you do not want to. Don't be fooled by their false and unwilling help which was shown in order to get something valuable in return.

False Assent

Closely related to this is how they act during a disagreement. During a disagreement, the abusive person gives assent to get you to back down. However, their point of view haven't changed.

In a normal relationship, people change their stance once they begin to see and understand the other person's point of view. But when the relationship is a toxic one, a yes is actually a no. Once you remind them of their consent at a later date, they will deny they ever agreed in the first place. This is why there are unwilling helpers, anyway.

The Foot-in-the-Door Tactics

"Could you donate $5 towards eradicating water pollution?" "Can I have your contact details for our monthly newsletters?"

The Foot-in-the-Door is a compliance tactic that manipulators use to get you agreeing to a small request first; and then agreeing to a larger request. Once you encourage a small gift or sacrifice, you create a bond which they exploit to extract greater compliance. This is a very subtle tactic that originates from salesmen who make door to door sales pitches. Once the door is open to hear them out, they jam a foot in it to prevent it from closing, while they make their pitch.

You agree to carry out an easy action or concede to a small demand like, *"Can I use your car to go to the store?"* and once you agree, you hear the larger request, "Can *I borrow it for the weekend?"* By getting you to concede to the first request, you are likely to concede to the second as well.

This tactic is based on the principle that a small agreement establishes a bond between two people, and the more you agree to minor or trivial requests and commitments, the more you will keep conceding to a higher request, especially along the same subject. It also works because people want to be consistent. If they are convinced that their initial agreement to a request or cause is a good one, they'll want to act consistently concerning the next, of similar subject. So the artful manipulator makes a small request, and a larger request follows soon after; knowing that their requests are likely to be agreed on, complied with or accepted.

Consider the common street request *"do you have the time?* And then the larger request "I *need $10 for a taxi"*. It becomes harder to say no, once you've said yes.

Another angle to this tactic is to do something nice and then immediately ask for something in return: "*I made dinner! Oh, and honey can you do all my laundry while I watch TV?"*

Denial

"I never said that!"

Emotional abusers may agree to a fact and then later deny it. This action is deliberate. For instance, a person may accept to take a particular position in a non-governmental association but when the demands of the new office starts to its toil, he/ she may deny ever agreeing to take the position in the first place.

The covert-aggressor could also use denial to intentionally get others to back off or back down or to make them feel guilty about their suggestions and hints.

What to do: if in a relationship with such a manipulator, he or she will never change. People who refuse to admit their wrongs in the first place will not feel any inclination to address them. You may have to walk away from such relationship, if you can no longer bear it. But if it occurs at your workplace, take note of this person and document/ record your discussions and negotiations.

Moving The Goal Post

"Yes, but…"

Narcissists do not want to help you improve. They simply want to pull you down and make a scapegoat of you as much as possible. They love to be continuously dissatisfied with you so they *move the goal post*. They set expectations of you and keep raising the bar, even after meeting previous demands. They also demand more proof of a successful action or experience you may have taken or undergone.

If you're a successful career person, they'll point out that you aren't a millionaire yet. If you made a fuss over their sprained ankle, you need to be *'stronger and more matured'*. The goal post is always being shifted even though these posts may be unrelated to each other. What the narcissist really want is for you to constantly seek their validation and approval.

Each time the manipulator raises their expectations of you, they manage to instil a sense of unworthiness that you carry everywhere, as well as a strong feeling of discontentment. They emphasize a minor fact or an error you made and focus their attention on these. As a result, they pull you away from your strengths and get you thinking and mulling over your flaws or weaknesses.

Moving the goal post will never end until you come to a realization that in spite of your wins and victories, you aren't being treated specially or celebrated. You have to understand that you are merely at the whims of the manipulator.

What to do: Once you notice that someone seems bent on reemphasizing and highlighting your irrelevant point repeatedly, to the extent they do not acknowledge the good work you've done. Realize that they simply want you to feel that you constantly have to prove yourself to them. So validate yourself and do not let anyone make you feel unworthy in any way.

<u>Triangulation</u>

"I wish you'd be a little more like her!"

Triangulation is when another's perspective, opinion, or suggested threat is brought into an ongoing interaction. To validate their toxic abuse, emotional abusers recourse to a third party: an ex-girlfriend, a female colleague at work, or an admirable relative, just to knock you off balance and make you insecure. They can even go as far as comparing you to a complete stranger! Also, they love to point out that that someone else, usually someone you know, agrees with or shares their point of view.

You'll hear statements like *"He wants me back, I really don't know what to do".* The narcissist uses this tactic to present a false image of themselves and make you compete for their attention. You also end up questioning yourself on your beliefs and stance. However, the abuser is often wrong. They love to report falsehood, especially on what others say or think about you. But in reality, they are the ones smearing you. They just want to confuse you and trouble you unnecessary.

For example, an abusive parent might ask family members to remind a child how much the parent has sacrificed for the child. The social pressure may convince the child to stop complaining about abusive behavior.

What to do: Gain support from any third party that is not under the narcissist's influence. Seek your own validation.

<u>**Slander**</u>

Manipulators are masters at deception. They discredit other people and invalidate their claims of truth. If they cannot control you, they will strive to control how other people see you. This is why they'll carry out a smear campaign to slander your name and dent your reputation. They aim to destroy your support network so they'll be nothing for you to fall back on in the event of a breakup or fallout.

They use one person to lie to the other and then use these two people to lie to a third. They ensure there is a distance among the people they slander so they cannot easily meet. But it may not be all lies. In most cases, they mix part of the truth with lies so that if they are discovered, they can focus on that little bit of truth.

Most people in a toxic relationship with a narcissist are usually unaware of the malicious statements made against them. So when the relationship ends, they are shocked to learn that such level of falsehoods were perpetrated against them. Toxic people gossip, tell stories about you to their friends and family, and even to yours. These stories label you as the aggressor and they, as the victim. They accuse you to others of engaging in a particular behavior, but they are the ones guilty of that behavior. They watch your reactions when they methodically, deliberately and covertly abuse you in order to use these reactions against you.

What to do: Mind your reactions and stick to the facts. If the toxic abuse persists, divorce is inevitable, if married. In that case, ensure

you document any harassment or stalking and speak with your
partner only through a lawyer.

<u>**False Guilt**</u>

"I thought I could count on you!"

Emotional manipulators use your feelings against you. They appeal to their victim's conscience so that they will have doubts, be anxious and be docile. They know how to make you feel guilty for the things you do or do not do. They accuse you for instance, for not caring enough, being unreasonable or too selfish in order to make you feel bad and do what is needed, usually their suggestions, in order to expunge your guilt feelings.

There are people with strong guilt reflex. They grew up in restrictive environments where punishment was meted out for every wrong committed. Such people grow up to feel guilty about everything they do. Narcissists who meet these people can effectively make them feel guilty for refusing to act as they want, until they succumb to their desires.

This is a false guilt used to manipulate: If someone won't do what you want, make them feel guilty. There are other examples such as:

"If you really loved me, you'd never question me."

"If you can't be here this weekend, I think it shows your level of dedication to this office."

"I've always been of great help to you and now you can't even do this little thing I ask?"

"Don't you want to donate money to help the starving children in Africa?

What to do: minimize your exposure to such guilty statements. Ignore manipulative words and do not respond to them.

<u>Shaming</u>

"You should be ashamed of yourself!"

… the Narcissists say often, tearing away at someone's self-esteem. Once they get to know you have suffered an injustice or abuse as a child, they will use this knowledge to shame you. For example, they may say that you brought it upon yourself. They could even talk about their own happy childhood in a boastful and proud way to make you feel unworthy.

Covert-aggressive manipulators use subtle sarcasm and rhetorical comments to make others feel unworthy or inadequate.

What to do: Unless you are talking with a professional or a trusted family with a proven character, do not reveal your past traumas or vulnerabilities. There is no point doing so and having them used against you in future.

Making Jokes at Your Expense

"Geez, you look exhausted!"

They say something rude or mean, but tell you they were just joking. They disguise sharp remarks as sarcasm or humor. They pretend to joke, but in reality, they want to make you feel doubtful and insecure. You can tell by the sadistic gleam and derisive smirk in their eyes that these covert narcissists enjoy these harmful remarks at your expense. They maintain a cool, innocent demeanor and when you point out how hurtful these remarks are; they will divert, gaslight and call out your perceived sensitivity.

What to do: This verbal abuse is demeaning and should not be encouraged. Stand up for yourself and categorically state that these type of behavior won't be tolerated.

Intimidation

If you are easily frightened or cajoled, you may be subject to intimidation by an abuser. They use intimidation, alongside bullying to get their demands met. They make weighty demands and insist that you do it the want they want. Intimidation can also be physical. If someone is considerably bigger, or stronger than you, they may stand over you in a threatening posture in order to intimidate and threaten you. But since we are talking about emotional manipulation here, we should point out that intimidation generally occurs when someone else is forced to accommodate an accuser's desire because acting on the contrary will make the abuser angry and aggressive.

Rationalization (Justification)

Justification or rationalization is the excuse a manipulator tries to provide for engaging in an inappropriate behavior. There is always an explanation for every action that they carry out which they use to convince you. It is called justification because the internal resistance that that should be felt due to an action or its consequence is removed, and in its place, there is justification for that action. The abuser is therefore free to pursue personal goals without external resistance and interference.

<u>**Isolation/ Home Court Advantage**</u>

"Walk over to my office. I'm far too busy to walk all the way over to you."

Manipulative people always want to place you in unfamiliar environments, which are familiar to them. They take a person out of their elements to their own favorite spots and places, including among their own friends. This is manipulative because they get you living their lives while they do not live yours in any way.

Of course there are instances where people want you to meet them where they are at. But it's manipulation when they want you to come to them all the time, even when they could easily come to you. In fact, they never seem to want to come to you.

Being in your home turf is really empowering. When you aren't comfortable in your surroundings, you are easier to control. This is why manipulators love this tactic as it is an easy way to gain control by taking up your time and demonstrating that they are in charge.

What to do: now you know; insist on meeting in your own environments and among your own friends and family. If it's work-related, offer to meet in a neutral space. It is important that you stay connected to your larger social circles. Manipulators cannot work effectively if you are surrounded by family and friends as they would want to pull you away in isolation.

Offering The Illusion Of Choice

"Go now or later?"

A common covert tactics that manipulates use is to offer you several choices that'll lead to the same result, whichever option you go for, you get the same exact outcome.

Bosses, and salespeople use this favorite technique e.g. *"Would you like the 6-month payment plan or pay it all right now up front?"*

It's just like flipping a coin that says *"Heads I win, tails you lose"*.

Using Non-Verbal Signs

Manipulators love using nonverbal signs to express themselves. These non-verbal signs are all negative. Head shaking, eyes rolling or sighing to express their disapproval or disappointment. This makes you doubt yourself and feel less confident. Non-verbal signs from someone that you care about like your parents, husband, wife; or someone with authority over you leaves you with a feeling of guilt and shame.

Intentional Misrepresentation

"So, you are saying I'm a bad person?"

Toxic people love to shift blame and distract attention from their own behavior. One of the ways they do this is to make your opinions, emotions and experiences look absurd or outrightly evil by translating these thoughts into character flaws and emphasizing their supposed irrationality.

They reframe your statements by putting words into your mouth. For instance, while recounting your day at work, you come to the part about your obnoxious colleagues and what they said to you. They'll cut you short saying *"Oh, so now you're perfect?"*

It's hard to express your feelings with such people because they put words into your mouth and jump to the wrong conclusions. They make you feel guilty for the thoughts and emotions you have about someone else's inappropriate behavior.

They believe they are good mind- readers and habitually jump into conclusions. Their actions are based on their own fallacies, delusions and triggers and even if they see that they've caused some harm, they make no apologies about it. They portray your viewpoint as outlandish and accuse you of depicting them as toxic even when you are yet to talk to them about their behavior.

What to do: simply say *"I never said that"* and walk away. Refrain from profuse defense.

False Anger

"I'M REALLY MAD THIS TIME!"

Manipulators feign anger to keep others off their backs. The feigned anger is usually intense because it is intended to shock you into submission. They put on this act whenever they are confronted with an issue so they can avoid revealing the truth. They also want their intention to remain hidden. So if you are someone who is easily frightened with anger, they will use it against you and then you find yourself giving in, sacrificing your desires and wants for theirs.

However, if you are strong enough to resist their feigned anger, they will unexpectedly switch to a lighter and joyous mood. You are relieved and prone to agree to the next request that is made. This is negative reinforcement. Anger is used to covertly manipulate you to avoid confrontation and remain submissive and subservient.

What to do: Pause and hold on for a moment before you react. Alternatively, walk away for a few minutes.

False Servitude

A nurturing, and caring act may not be to your best interests. People who say they have your best interest at heart while they do things for you make it difficult for you to fault their bad behavior. They claim it is for your good or for the good of humanity or the general society. This may not be true.

A wife repeatedly pushes her husband to take a promotion he doesn't like or feel inclined to. The wife claims it is to create a higher living standard for the children and family, but the reluctant husband isn't happy about it. Since he cannot actually find fault in her claim, he will ultimately accept her rationalization of the situation but will still feel bad that he hates his new job. This tactic is difficult to recognize because on the surface it is servitude but underneath the primary aim is dominance.

<u>**Intellectual Bullying**</u>

"I know these are a lot of numbers for you, so I'll go through this again slowly."

You ask a simple question and you are inundated with statistics jargon, large words or arrogant sentences which are presented in a condescending way. This is the tactic manipulators who want to be seen as expert and an authority figure utilize. Known as intellectual bullying, it is similar to what salesman do to get you to buy their products.

Manipulators therefore, will include fake facts, flashy words and technical details in subjects you have little knowledge about, knowing that you may not have the opportunity to verify these claims. For that reason, they place themselves as an authority of some sort in order for you could feel inferior while they exert their dominance and control over you.

What to do: Once they get into their intellectual bullying discourse, tune out. Respectfully say: *"thank you, but this isn't a discussion I want to have."*

<u>**The Fear-Then-Relief Tactics**</u>

"I know it must be pretty hard to meet people when you are working and putting a lot into your career. I understand. There are several women in my company like that who ended up alone with cats as companion…   my friends and I will be going for a really cool party. You are welcome to join us, if you want to"

"Management is considering lying off a few staff, you know, there's so much to do and very low revenue…just saying…that reminds me, would you be willing to work overtime all through the week?"

The abuser issues a threat that places you in fear; almost immediately, he removes this threat and replaces it with a mild request. The fear comes with a lot of stress and anxiety and you are immediately relieved that it is over. You have experienced a mood cycle that is likely to disarm you, making it difficult for you to resist their offer.

What to do: Do not respond immediately. Tell the manipulator to give you a few minutes to think about it.

The Negative Out-doer

"You think that's bad? My cube-mate talks on the phone all the time."

"Be thankful you have a brother. I've felt alone all my life."

The negative out-doer will diminish your problems and play up their own, so you can never outshine them. If you have a bad day, they've had it worse. If you start to talk about just how bad it's been, you are curtly interrupted and presented with a detailed account of their rough day, making yours seem so trivial. They negate your statements by outdoing you. So if you have a headache, theirs will be a brain tumor! It is only when you bring up your problem that they remember they have theirs; which is usually worse.

They have a way of turning conversations around and putting the spotlight back on themselves. The aim is to simply invalidate your experiences to get you focused on them and exert your emotional energy on their problems.

Similar to this is exaggeration. Every situation you've been through, they can relate as they've had it 10 times worse! They want to be the focus of attention and gain the upper hand by distancing themselves from you. Fortunately, it is easy to spot by the watchful even after frequent denials.

What to do: say *"that may be true, but we'll get to yours later"*.

Typecasting

"You come from a well-off family, you couldn't possibly understand what it's like to be poor.'

Deliberately using negative labels to get you to react in the opposite direction. Striving to change your behavior in order to prove someone wrong might be a form of manipulation.

What to do: To ensure you do not fall to this tactic, make a conscious decision about how you want to act depending on what the particular behavior is and the things happening around you.

Disguised Questions

"I suppose you are going to..."

Manipulators hate asking questions for they feel it may make them lose control. Instead, they disguise their questions as statements. For examples: *"I wish you could..."*, *"I am wondering why you..."*

What to do: work on recognizing the difference between a direct question and a disguised question. Force the manipulator to admit it was a question by repeating the statement back to him or her. Once clarified, answer only a direct question.

Unsolicited Promises

"I'll pay you back, I promise."

"I promise I will never lie to you."

"I promise... I promise"

What to do: Ensure that the person you intend to commit your personal or emotional safety to has a proven history of keeping promises. Remember that abusers lie and exaggerate; therefore making constant unsolicited promises before or after every statement is a red flag.

Belittling Your Opinions

"Don't be silly"

"You're being ridiculous"

Some skilled manipulators won't say anything overtly cruel. However, they will use a gentle tone and language to make you feel anything but adorable. You leave a conversation feeling as though a part of your dignity and respect went with it. You won't be able to really pinpoint why you are feeling kind of goofy.

The sneaky character has just used the opportunity to patronize you, placing themselves as the one with the experience, expertise and perspective that you can trust. They simply want to create an uneven playing field, where they are the dominant one who should be looked up to. This happens in relationships, family and the workplace. Recognize it and ensure that you do not give power to this manipulator under the guise of providing advice, counselling or leadership.

A regular person with no manipulative tendencies will speak to you as an equal. They will respect your strengths, understand your weakness and never belittle in private or in public. They will share their wisdom freely and happily without getting overly upset or controlling even when you do not take their advice.

A manipulator is upset when you do not take their advice. They may manage to keep their anger and frustration in check but will place pressure on you to do exactly what they suggest. Soon, you may begin to feel that you can't make good decisions on your own and you'll be consider depending on them for accurate perspective.

The Sympathetic Approach

"Trust me, you're in safe hands"

Toxic and abusive people like to show that they are very compassionate. At the beginning of your relationship, they will carry out a high level of sympathy to dupe you. After a while, they will unveil their mask and you'll see a callous, contemptuous and cold person beneath.

How do you detect false sympathy and compassion? Manipulative people often want to reassure you of their trust, even when the friendship or relationship is new.

Emotional manipulators often attempt to establish intimacy early in a relationship by sharing deep and deep personal information that is mostly untrue. They do this to bridge the trust barrier so that once they share something very private and personal with you, you will begin to feel sorry for them and see them as emotionally open, very sensitive and a little vulnerable.

The information they share will be relevant to you. Watch out! It is a tactic to get you to trust them and equally confide something very personal. Eventually, they will use the personal information you shared with them to hurt or manipulate you.

Chapter Three

How To Stop Being Manipulated

Having recognized that you are being manipulated, the next step is to stop the manipulation outrightly. This is the difficult past; but, it is possible to stop being a victim of manipulation, regardless of how long it has been.

1. **Be Open Minded.** There is what is known as exhortation and what is known as manipulation. Ask yourself if your choices are really yours; or the other persons. Are you being made to act the way this person wants, thereby overriding your choices. It is manipulation when everything is done solely for the other's benefit. However, if someone speaks the truth to you but leaves you to go ahead with your decision, accepting and respecting your final judgment, despite having a contrary view, this is exhortation and it's spoken sincerely for your benefit.

Understand when manipulation is normal and when it's not. There are times when people simply make manipulative or passive-aggressive comments. But it ends there. Manipulation becomes an issue when it's abusive, more problematic and steered towards controlling or harming another.

At the point of detecting manipulation, tell the other person exactly how you want to be treated and then stick to your own guideline. For instance, *"Mom, I appreciate how you sacrificed so much for me, but you don't*

Do not accept an insincere apology. How do you know that it is insincere? It feels like bullshit! This is where you have to trust your guts and senses. The manipulator is searching for a tactic; a maneuver and if you yield, it will become a steady part of the bull you are being fed.

2. **Set Healthy Boundaries And Enforce Them**. Keep yourself from harm by enforcing boundaries. The boundary must be as stronger than the manipulator's destructive tendencies. Begin by avoiding calls and text messages and act as if you are really very busy. Make it seem unintentional. The lesser time the manipulator spends with you, the better for your sanity. Besides, it leaves the manipulator helpless.

3. **See A Licensed Counselor Or Therapist**. There may be hidden personal issues in your life that needs addressing. A license counselor is objective and will help you identify them, and guide you on the best ways to interact with the manipulator. A therapist who understands personality disorders can also offer tremendous help.

Confrontation is the best way to tackle disagreements between two people. But confronting a person one-on-one may not always work. If the person is not physically, emotionally and verbally safe enough for confronting, the resultant negative backlash will worsen the situation. This is where you need your counselor's input.

If the other party is willing, a therapist can work with everyone (families and couples) to help them build healthier communication patterns and get their needs met safely and happily. Seeing a therapist will help to break free from the manipulation and also help you reduce the risk of being trapped in such manipulative relationship again.

You can also talk to a trusted friend, a close family and in extreme fearful situations, the police.

4. **Love Yourself**

Your top priorities should be self-care and self-love. You must stand up for yourself and identify signs of a potentially unhealthy relationship or friendship. Take time to think about the signs that you spot, listen to your intuition and do the right thing.

5. **Time To Say Goodbye**

There is no need staying in a toxic manipulative relationship or friendship. If you've done your best to speak to the other party and all you get is defense and reluctance to hear you out or change, then best thing is to walk out of the friendship or relationship. It's important that you safeguard yourself, your happiness is important, do not allow someone else make you feel bad about yourself. Terminate the contact if necessary then immediately keep company with people who value you and treat you with respect and honor.

Concluded